Bonds of Fear

Joni Eareckson Tada

ROSE PUBLISHING/ASPIRE PRESS

Torrance, California

Breaking the Bonds of Fear
© Copyright 2014 Joni Eareckson Tada

Aspire Press, an imprint
of Rose Publishing, Inc.
4733 Torrance Blvd., #259
Torrance, California 90503 USA
www.rose-publishing.com
www.aspirepress.com

Printed by Regent Publishing Services Ltd.
Printed in China
December 2013, 1st printing

Contents

The Author

Joni Eareckson Tada, the founder and chief executive officer of Joni and Friends International Disability Center, is an international advocate for people with disabilities. A diving accident in 1967 left Joni Eareckson, then 17,  a quadriplegic in a wheelchair. After two years of rehabilitation, she emerged with new skills and a fresh determination to help others in similar situations. She founded Joni and Friends in 1979 to provide Christ-centered programs to special needs families, as well as training to churches. Through the organization's *Christian Institute on Disability*, Joni and her team have helped develop disability ministry courses of study in major Christian universities and seminaries. Visit us at www.joniandfriends.org.

Where Does Fear Come From?

I was your typical insecure teenager sitting in my high school social sciences class and listening to a lecture on how humans react to fear. The teacher summed up our instinctual response to fear in three words: "Flight or fight." I recall thinking, *No wonder I'm so worn out! I'm constantly afraid of what other people think of me… I'm nervous that no one will ask me to the sophomore dance… I'm afraid I'll fail my chemistry test… I'm afraid I won't make the varsity basketball team.* It seemed that half my life was spent avoiding certain people and situations (flight) or struggling to make the grade or meet someone's expectations (fight). I was only in tenth grade, but already I was emotionally worn to the core.

Joni at 15

They say that the number one menace to world health is not cancer, AIDS, plagues, or polio. It's stress. Stress has its root in what we fear. When it comes to handling fear, it seems that humans can only take so much "flight or fight"—it results in pressure, nervous tension, worry, and anxiety. But what is at the real root of fear itself?

> "Worry is like a rocking chair—it keeps you moving but doesn't get you anywhere."
> —Corrie ten Boom

Fear of Man

"Fear of man will prove to be a snare, but whoever trusts in the Lord is kept safe."
—Proverbs 29:25

What does it mean to have a fear of man? Although you can be an avowed worshiper of the true God, below the surface, the real "god" can be others around you. To fear man includes being afraid of someone, but it also means holding someone in awe, or being controlled or mastered by the opinions of others, or putting all your trust in people, or needing others to an unhealthy extent. In short, you replace God with people. The fear of man goes by other names, too. Teenagers call it "peer pressure"; adults call it "people-pleasing;" psychologists label it "codependency."

How do you know if you possess a fear of man?

† Do you "paint on a smile" or "put on a front" when you're among those you want to impress? Are you afraid of being exposed as an imposter?

† How much do you "need" your spouse? Unless you have a grasp of the biblical parameters of marital commitment and responsibility, your spouse may become the one you fear, controlling you and quietly taking the place of God in your life.

† Do you revere or fear others' opinions, needing them to buttress your sense of well-being and identity?

† Are you afraid of making mistakes that will make you look bad in the eyes of others? Do you find it hard to say no even when wisdom dictates that you should? Are you on too many committees at church? You could be a people-pleaser.[1]

Fear of the Lord

"*The fear of the LORD* leads to life: Then one rests content, untouched by trouble." —Proverbs 19:23

Fear of the Lord:

Reverent submission that leads to obedience

Virtually all of our worry and stress could be alleviated if we understood how to exchange "fear of man" for "fear of the Lord." We need a way to think less often about ourselves and more often about God. "God must be bigger to you than people are," writes Edward Welch in his book, *When People are Big and God is Small*. When it comes to our family and friends, coworkers and neighbors, our problem is sometimes that we *need* them (and their approval) for ourselves more than we *love* them for the glory of God. The task God sets for us in life is to emotionally "require" people *less* and to love them *more*.

To escape the fear of man is to recognize that *God* is the One who is awesome and glorious, not other people. We need to understand and grow in the fear of the Lord—because the person who fears God will fear nothing else!

What Is the Fear of the Lord?

The fear of the Lord includes a spectrum of attitudes. In one sense, it does indeed mean a terror of God; for we are unclean people who will one day appear before the Almighty, who is holy and morally pure. Such fear shrinks back from God. But for people whose eyes have been opened to God's great love, this terror-fear gradually fades the more we come to know him.

For those who have put their faith in Jesus Christ, fear of the Lord means *reverent submission that leads to obedience.* Yes, such reverence includes an awareness of our sinfulness and God's holiness, but it is balanced by the knowledge of God's great forgiveness, mercy, and love. A proper fear of the Lord will have us moving from terror, dread, and trembling, toward devotion, adoration, and enjoyment of God. This is the love 1 John 4:18 is speaking of when it says, "There is no fear [terror or dread] in love."[2]

When we trust in Christ, we are able to truly love other people—not to need or fear them, worry about them, or people-please them. We are able to:

† Love our enemies and pray for them

† Think about the needs of our spouse before our own needs

† Walk into a room and not worry about others' opinions of us

† Say no to others without fear of judgment

† Walk into church and feel like we're with family—with the family of God, there is no self-consciousness, embarrassment, or fear

Proverbs on the Fear of the Lord

The book of Proverbs shows us that the fear of the Lord is a great treasure. Many proverbs display the priceless value of the fear of God.

- † Those who fear the Lord will fear nothing else (see Prov. 19:23).

- † The fear of the Lord adds length to life (see Prov. 10:27).

- † The fear of the Lord is a secure fortress for the one who fears and for his or her children (see Prov. 14:26).

- † The fear of the Lord is a fountain of life (see Prov. 14:27).

- † The fear of the Lord should be praised when we see it (see Prov. 31:30).

What does the fear of the Lord look like? It looks like loving good and hating evil. It looks like trusting God, having reverence for him and obeying him.

† To fear the Lord is to hate evil (Prov. 8:13).

Your Security and Significance: A Personal Perspective

A woman once said to me, "Joni, you seem so confident. You seem to fear nothing. Have you always been that way?" Inwardly I smiled. If she only knew the knots I feel in my stomach before I speak to a crowd, or the times I'm scared stiff to sit in front of a blank canvas with a paintbrush. If she only knew the times I lay awake at night worrying about deadlines, or fretting that my words offended a coworker.

I have a long way to go before my "fear of man" is exchanged for a healthy "fear of God." For me, it started in my childhood scramble to keep up with three older, more athletic sisters. As a four-year-old, I would cling to the saddle horn as my sixteen-hands-high horse galloped behind the steeds of my sisters. I didn't dare tell them how scared I was!

My life journey has been to put aside those insecurities. And my wheelchair has helped. At first, my affliction made me feel more insecure. Over the years God has used my quadriplegia to force me to sit still, quit competing and comparing, and be quiet before him. People are only as secure as the source of their security; if we are secure in Christ, then we have every reason to be confident.

Psychologists say that good mental health springs from two things: security and significance. We find security in *who we are* and significance in *what we do*. Acts 17:28 says, "For in him we live and move and have our being." Since Christ is the source of peace, joy, strength, and rest, and in him we live and move and have our very being, we can be secure and feel significant when we place our trust in Jesus.

"If you look at the world, you'll be distressed. If you look within, you'll be depressed. If you look at God you'll be at rest." —Corrie ten Boom

Who we are: As Christians, we are free from the power of sin. We are children of God and co-heirs with Christ.

What we do: As Christians, we are free to truly love others and serve the Lord. We have a specific role to play in the advancement of Christ's kingdom on earth.

> *Lord, there are so many times when I feel afraid and insecure. Today I recognize that in you I live, move, and have my being—my life is secure because I am your child; my life is significant because you have a service for me to do.*

Worry

Jesus was talking to his disciples who had left their jobs to follow him:

"Therefore I tell you, do not worry about your life, what you will eat or drink; or about your body, what you will wear. Is not life more important than food, and the body more important than clothes? Look at the birds of the air. Are you not much more valuable than they? Who of you by worrying can add a single hour to his life? And why do you worry about clothes? See how the lilies of the field grow. So do not worry, saying, 'What shall we eat?' or 'What shall we drink?' or 'What shall we wear?' But seek first his kingdom and his righteousness, and all these things will be given to you as well. Therefore do not worry about tomorrow, for tomorrow will worry about itself. Each day has enough trouble of its own" (Matt. 6:25–28, 31, 33–34).

Go back over these verses and count how many times the Lord uses the word *worry*. Talk about driving home a point!

The Lord was wise in repeating his warning so many times. He knows the devastating effects of worrying and how it can corrode your confidence in God like acid. Worry robs you of joy, and it steals your hope. What is worrying you today? A deadline or a diet? A car payment or a gloomy medical report? Repeat your reading of Matthew 6:25–34 and personalize it by putting your name after each time the Lord commands (notice, it's not a suggestion): "Do not worry."

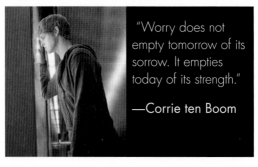

"Worry does not empty tomorrow of its sorrow. It empties today of its strength."

—Corrie ten Boom

Lord, I admit that I'm so prone to worrying about things that happen in my life. Help me today to trust you. Receive glory as I turn from my anxiety and turn to you. Thank you that Jesus has given me this solemn warning not to worry.

"To carry worry to bed is to sleep with a pack on your back."

—Thomas Haliburton

Fear and Anxiety: You're Not the Only One!

It happens to the best of us. Your calendar gets crowded with obligations and appointments; you look at your budget and worry about maxing out before month's end; your insurance company turns down your renewal; and your car needs extra repairs. When one thing piles on top of the next, it's hard not to listen to fear knocking at your door. We live in a fast-paced world that almost every day pushes us to the edge of anxiety.

But draw encouragement from the apostle Paul. He understands the problem! After all, the man who called himself "the chief of sinners" also struggled with worry and anxiety. Look at what Paul writes in Philippians 2:28. He's talking about sending

Epaphroditus, his fellow worker, to the church in Philippi, and he writes, "Therefore I am all the more eager to send him, so that when you see him again you may be glad and *I may have less anxiety*" [italics mine]. Paul—the great apostle, the writer of most of the New Testament—dealt with anxiety?! Yes. Which makes what Paul has to say about anxiety a few chapters later all the more meaningful. Paul may have struggled with anxiety, but he gives us the tools to deal with it.

"Leave tomorrow's trouble to tomorrow's strength; tomorrow's work to tomorrow's time; tomorrow's trial to tomorrow's grace and to tomorrow's God."

—James Russell Lowell

You may know Philippians 4:6–7 by heart: "Do not be anxious about anything, but in everything, by prayer and petition, with thanksgiving, present your requests to God. And the peace of God, which transcends all understanding, will guard your hearts and your minds in Christ Jesus." This powerful verse is your antidote to worry. But what makes this verse so special, so potent? It's Philippians 4:5, the verse right before it: "The Lord is near."

The Antidote to Worry

The Lord is near! This fundamental truth provides the foundation for Philippians 4:6. You could read it this way: "The Lord is near, so do not be anxious about anything. The Lord is near, so in everything, feel comfortable about presenting your requests to him." You can go through *anything*; you can sit with slumped shoulders next to the hospital bedside of a loved one, facing a most fearsome future, and do so without worrying—*if* you are convinced the Lord is standing next to you. And he is. Philippians 4:5 tells you so.

In Philippians 4:6, prayer is mentioned three times.

The answer to anxiety and fear? Pray, pray, pray!

In Philippians 4:7, we are assured that the peace of God will chase away fear and safeguard our hearts and minds in calm-centeredness in Christ.

"Courage is fear that has said its prayers."
—Dorothy Bernard

Jesus Is the Ballast in Your Ship

"All the waters in all the oceans cannot sink a ship... nor can all the trouble in all the world harm us unless it gets within us."
—Eugene Peterson

If you're like me, you have a certain respect for the troubles that come your way. Let me be honest. I have lived more than 45 years as a spinal cord injured quadriplegic—I'm breaking all the statistics that say I should be dead (which makes me extremely respectful of each healthy day I enjoy). It is *amazing* that I possess such a hale and hearty constitution.

But fears can creep in and destroy my peace of mind. Sometimes I allow myself to reflect upon all the trouble I *could* be experiencing. Breaking one of my already-fragile bones… bladder bugs…lung infections…pressure sores…the growing specter of blood clots… uncontrollable spasticity. These are the kinds of troubles most quadriplegics wrestle with all the time. So if I let my fears get "within me," as the quotation above says, I'd be sunk! I'd be flooded with fear. I'd drown in anxiety and worry.

"Never be afraid to trust an unknown future to a known God."
—Corrie ten Boom

It's why I take great comfort in Eugene Peterson's advice. *All* the waters in all of the oceans cannot sink a ship. It is completely safe as long as no water from the ocean gets inside it. If that occurs, the ship is doomed. In the same way, all the troubles in the entire world cannot touch me, *unless* I allow them to get inside me. I'm safe as long as I do not allow fear or worry to sink my heart, submerge my peace of mind or plunge my joy into a flood of despair.

As long as Jesus is the ballast in my ship, I am *safe*. After all, he said in John 16:33, "In this world you will have trouble. But take heart! I have overcome the world."

Ballast:

Heavy material, such as sand or lead, placed low in a vessel to give stability.

Ballast from God's Word

When I fill my vessel with promises like these, the waters of my troubles can't sink me!

† Even though I walk through the valley of the shadow of death, I will fear no evil, for you are with me; your rod and your staff, they comfort me. —Psalm 23:4

† The Lord himself goes before you and will be with you; he will never leave you nor forsake you. Do not be afraid; do not be discouraged. —Deuteronomy 31:8

† [Jesus said,] "Peace I leave with you; my peace I give you. I do not give to you as the world gives. Do not let your hearts be troubled and do not be afraid." —John 14:27

† Do not be anxious about anything, but in everything, by prayer and petition, with thanksgiving, present your requests to God. And the peace of God, which transcends all understanding, will guard your hearts and your minds in Christ Jesus. —Philippians 4:6–7

† Cast all your anxiety on him because he cares for you. —1 Peter 5:7

"I'm Afraid to Share my Faith!"

Candy told me about a dinner party she attended recently where one of the guests, an agnostic, was sitting across from her. The discussion turned to politics and ethics. Candy saw an opening to steer the conversation toward the gospel and wanted very much to say something, but she didn't. She rationalized that it wasn't her dinner party and she didn't want to create an embarrassing scene for the hostess. So Candy said nothing. Later on she confided that the *real* reason was plain old fear. She said, "Joni, I'm ashamed to say, I'm a coward when it comes to talking about my Christian faith."

I, too, have felt the same shame Candy experienced; I've also backed away and sidestepped obvious opportunities to share my faith. Looking back, I *know* the Holy Spirit set up those opportunities for me to give the gospel.

Of all the things that make our palms sweat and knees shake; of all the things that make our heart rates rise and our mouths go dry, it's witnessing to unbelievers about Jesus Christ and his claim on our lives. Most of us are good at dropping broad hints, or inviting a neighbor to a church event, but then we leave the rest to the Holy Spirit, hoping our neighbor will "get the hint." We have a hard time saying Jesus is the only way and he is your only escape from hell. Tough words, but God tells us not to be afraid of calling Christ our Lord and Savior.

Infuse courage into your convictions by musing over the following:

† Jesus wasn't embarrassed to take on your sin and mine; he was no coward going to the cross.

† Your Savior has the heart of a lion. Ask God to give you his heart for this lost world.

† Practice giving your testimony to a close friend. Memorize as much as you can so you won't be at a loss for words when asked about your faith.

† Courage breeds courage. Timidity and fear breed even more fear.

Spend time with people who are courageous for Christ, and it will inspire courage of your own convictions. "For God did not give us a spirit of timidity, but a spirit of power, of love and of self-discipline" (2 Tim. 1:7).

"The Bible is a firsthand story of goose-bump courage in very ordinary people who were invaded by the living God."
—Tim Hansel

"Pray I'll Have Courage!"

The apostle Paul may be considered one of the most bold and courageous ambassadors of the gospel, but even he got butterflies in his stomach. In one paragraph, he twice asks for prayer for courage in sharing the truth of the gospel. How odd to think that even the great apostle felt fear. But he asked his friends, "Pray

"Since there is no room in our hearts to worship both God and people, whenever people are big, God is not. Therefore, the first task in escaping the snare of the fear of man is to know that God is awesome and glorious, not other people."

—Edward T. Welch

also for me, that whenever I open my mouth, words may be given me *so that I will fearlessly make known the mystery of the gospel*, for which I am an ambassador in chains. *Pray that I may declare it fearlessly*, as I should" (Eph. 6:19–20).

Fear is natural for humans. Fearlessness is a supernatural grace God gives when we, like Paul, pray and ask for courage. We may fumble with what to say, when and how to say it; we may struggle with what to do, when and how to do it. That's why prayer is the best preface to either declaring or demonstrating the gospel. The Lord is our resource for courage.

Lord, I need your courage today. Help me to look for opportunities to make known your gospel. And when I open my mouth, please give me words so that I can fearlessly declare and demonstrate your gospel of love.

Death:
The Ultimate Fear

Remember the words to that old song, "I'm tired of living but scared of dying"? Ever since the days of Eden, people have been haunted by fears on each side of the grave. On this side of the tombstone, our fears are aggravated by pain and suffering. We anxiously think, *Will it always be this way? Will it get worse?* We long for relief and so look forward to the time when we will be free of pain and suffering—but when people try to peer beyond the grave, their anxieties are often aggravated by the unknown. We worry, *I'm afraid of getting older and of dying. It's so scary and... permanent!*

Jesus Christ, the Prince of Peace, is the only one who can rid you of fear, whether it's fear in the here and now or fear of the future. Peace is the opposite of fear.

A prescription for peace is found in Hebrews 2:14–15, "Since the children have flesh and blood, he too shared in their humanity so that by his death he might destroy him who holds the power of death—that is, the devil—and free those who all their lives were held in slavery by their fear of death."

Here's how it breaks down: God became a human being—that is, Jesus. Jesus, through his death, broke the power of the Devil and his lies. This same Jesus desires to deliver you of your fears, whether you're frightened of life as a living nightmare or fearing death as a scary unknown. To place your trust in Jesus gives you peace now and peace about the hereafter.

You no longer need to be afraid of living and scared of dying! To place your hand in the Prince of Peace's hand does not necessarily guarantee you protection from suffering.

But it does give you protection from fear, including a steadfast hand to hold onto and the certainty that a loving and all-powerful God who knows everything is standing by your side. Putting your confidence in Christ will free you from living all your life as a slave to constant dread.

My Brush with Death

Someone once heard about my diving accident and asked, "Joni, didn't you panic when you were face down in the water? You were running out of breath. Weren't you frightened?" Strange as it may seem, I wasn't frightened. Although I knew that in the next few seconds water would flood my lungs, a deep and powerful peace held fear at bay. Psalm 68:20 explains why: "Our God is a God who saves; from the Sovereign Lord comes escape from death."

Our sovereign Lord is an "escape artist" when it comes to death. "All that pertains to deliverance from death, all that prepares for it, all that makes it easy to be borne, all that constitutes a rescue from its pains and horrors, all that follows death in a higher and more blessed world, all that makes death 'final,' and places us in a condition where death is no more to be dreaded—all this belongs to God. All this is under his control. He only can enable us to bear death; he only can conduct us from a bed of death to a world where we shall never die."[3]

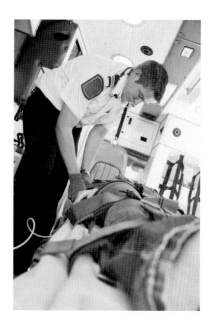

Psalm 18:4–6 says, *"The cords of death entangled me; the torrents of destruction overwhelmed me. The cords of the grave coiled around me; the snares of death confronted me. In my distress I called to the Lord; I cried to my God for help."*

As it turned out, my sister Kathy rescued me seconds before I began to drown.

Prince of Peace, forgive me for allowing fear to come between us. I have no need to fear what will happen today. I have no need to fear what will happen when I die. Free me to live every day without fear.

A Story from the Gospel of Mark

"That day when evening came, he said to his disciples, 'Let us go over to the other side.' Leaving the crowd behind, they took him along, just as he was, in the boat. There were also other boats with him. A furious squall came up, and the waves broke over the boat, so that it was nearly swamped. Jesus was in the stern, sleeping on a cushion. The disciples woke him and said to him, 'Teacher, don't you care if we drown?'" (Mark 4:35–38). Let's review what happened here…

† The disciples were overwhelmed by their frightening circumstances.

† Although the Lord of the universe was with them, they chose to focus on the danger rather than on his presence and help.

† The disciples were indignant that Jesus did not appear to care.

† Conclusion? The disciples were filled with doubts and fear.

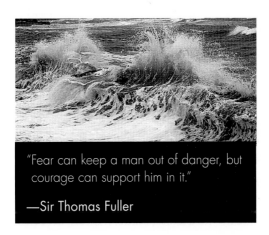

"Fear can keep a man out of danger, but courage can support him in it."

—Sir Thomas Fuller

Let's continue the story: "[Jesus] got up, rebuked the wind and said to the waves, 'Quiet! Be still!' Then the wind died down and it was completely calm. He said to his disciples, 'Why are you so afraid? Do you still have no faith?' They were terrified and asked each other, 'Who is this? Even the wind and the waves obey him!'" (Mark 4:39–41).

- † They discovered that Jesus cared deeply about their circumstances.

- † They witnessed firsthand God's awesome power.

- † Conclusion? The disciples were filled with a fear of the Lord.

Notice from the story in Mark that Jesus asked his followers a key question, "Why are you so afraid?" It's the same question God is asking you today. Please do not fight feelings of fear—it's a losing battle. Instead, deal with the reasons you have so many fears. See and believe that:

1. God is sovereign and in control of every circumstance that seems dangerous or "out of control" (Eph. 1:11).

2. God cares deeply about your plight (1 Peter 5:7).

3. God wants you to trust him as you cultivate a healthy awe, reverence, and respect for him (Isa. 33:6).

He will be the sure foundation for your times, a rich store of salvation and wisdom and knowledge; the fear of the Lord is the key to this treasure. —Isaiah 33:6

So do not fear, for I am with you; do not be dismayed, for I am your God. I will strengthen you and help you; I will uphold you with my righteous right hand. —Isaiah 41:10

Lord, I give you any anguish in my spirit, and I confess all my doubts and fears. I will exchange my fears for faith in you.

Notes:

1 Edward T. Welch, *When People Are Big and God is Small,* Puritan & Reformed Pub (New Jersey), 1997, p. 19

2 Ibid, p. 96–97.

3 Albert Barnes, *Notes, Critical, Explanatory, and Practical on the Psalms* (Psalm 68:20). New York: Harper & Brothers, 1869, vol. II, p. 213.

Books by Joni Eareckson Tada

The topics of fear and hopelessness, depression and suffering, loneliness and worry are issues that author Joni Eareckson Tada can speak to personally. Let Joni tell you her secrets to peace and joy. She knows that God does not take pleasure in seeing you suffer. He has compassion for you and gives you many ways to deal with life's pain so that you can have peace.

Making Sense of Suffering

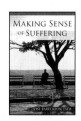

When you're overwhelmed by pain and problems, it's easy to feel helpless, hopeless, and sinking into a whirlpool of self-pity. Joni Eareckson Tada knows about these emotions first hand. Joni shares biblical insights that bring hope and comfort to those who are trying to make sense of their suffering.

Paperback, 4" x 6", 48 pages, ISBN 9781628620467

God's Hand in Our Hardship

When you read through the Bible, you can see that God hates suffering. So why doesn't our all-powerful God get rid of suffering? Joni Eareckson Tada tackles the big questions about suffering: How can a gracious and loving God allow anyone to suffer? Why do "good" people have to suffer? What possible good can come through suffering?

Paperback, 4"x 6", 48 pages, ISBN 9781628620474

Breaking the Bonds of Fear

Is fear causing you to lose sleep, stress out, and worry? When Joni Eareckson Tada experienced a tragic accident that left her quadriplegic, fear gripped her life. Joni explains the steps she took—and still takes daily—to grow in confidence in the Lord and break the bonds of fear.

Paperback, 4"x 6", 48 pages, ISBN 9781628620481

Prayer: Speaking God's Language

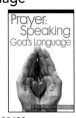

How can we draw closer to God in prayer? How can we "speak God's language"? As Christians grow in the discipline of praying, it becomes clear that there is always more to learn. Joni Eareckson Tada shares personal stories and insights that will help you hone your skill of praying with the Word of God.

Paperback, 4"x 6", 48 pages, ISBN 9781628620498

Available at www.aspirepress.com or wherever good Christian books are sold.